Other titles in the UWAP Poetry series (established 2016)

The Other Flesh contains many poems whose texture sings of being alone under the stars. It begins in stark paddocks with bleak greyhound runs, where Coburn's father has 'blood dripping from his fingers from feeding the dogs' and the poet responds with 'I love all the things I hate about being here', a line that brings Jack Spicer to mind. This poetry comes from tough experiences; yet Coburn's 'raw mind' creates an inner life that draws in the reader. We pass through a post-pastoral world and are pulled into a place where 'the self is only one version of hell'. We discover 'There is no fixed life form' on pages of empty skies and empty roads, empty fields of memory, with a throat full of toxin, eyes being bottled by 'sobered hands' and where road signs tell the poet what to do. Out of this abyss Coburn creates some beautiful lines, 'wind cutting through the tin' where 'dogs of sand' run beside him. When his grandfather dies of Parkinson's we come across this liberating image in the final line of the elegy: 'grasses that flow gently when all breath expires'. Coburn's world shimmers with light as much as it burns with ferocity but these finely written poems are free from bitterness or anger. Here are two lines that sit on the lyrical scales, being weighed for balance: 'the night sky is a blank, unbrushed canvas' and then 'a muteness that lies down in darkness'. When we open up Coburn's paddocks 'made up by the mind', they are transparent, and yet they are created with a muscular craft that glows with alert intelligence. These poems contain deep loss and wonder, informed by the anxieties involved with a longing to unite with the soul of the beloved. Coburn writes 'my flesh starved of paradise' – this book is a record of his successful call to regain it.

Robert Adamson

The Other Flesh

Robbie Coburn

Robbie Coburn's poetry has been published
in places such as *Poetry, Meanjin, Island* and
Westerly, and anthologised in *Writing to the Wire*
(UWA Publishing, 2016) and *To End All Wars*
(Puncher & Wattman, 2018). He lives on a farm
in Woodstock, Victoria.

Robbie Coburn
The Other Flesh

Poetry

First published in 2019 by
UWA Publishing
Crawley, Western Australia 6009
www.uwap.uwa.edu.au

UWAP is an imprint of UWA Publishing,
a division of The University of Western Australia.

Copyright © Robbie Coburn 2019
The moral right of the author has been asserted.
ISBN: 978-1-76080-098-7

A catalogue record for this
book is available from the
National Library of Australia

Designed by Becky Chilcott, Chil3
Typeset in Lyon Text by Lasertype
Printed by McPherson's Printing Group

uwapublishing

For Charles Buckmaster

Contents

Remembering is only a new form of suffering.

Charles Baudelaire

Suicide Country

Suicide Country

Been here too long, have to get out
the fear that beats into you
living in the country remains with you long after you've gone
becoming a second skin dislodged when away from the grasses

a part of the body embedded in endless paddocks
from the beginning, the greater years convene
at the point of youth
threads of a silence beckoning you nearer –

the farmland has its own language, the voice of dirt you numb with
    drink,
with marks along your flesh that never heal, only press deeper

you learn too late, never escaping the clean wind
inside the fence lines, the property's border
fleeing from all you know to be consuming

to get out, take a rifle from the shed and do away
with the isolation for good, is all you can dream of
where the air stands in place of buildings,
with no-one new to see
freedom becomes intolerable
that's why more people die by their own hand
in the country than in the cold city

everyone is somehow absent of themselves
when isolation is your company,
the quiet land without immersion

the road out of town that rises beneath cars
leaving the country for the city
your feet never miss the paddocks,
though still a tension between the outside
and the openness.

Learning the Paddock Scripture

In the paddock you map the structure of your breath. it traverses
the grasses – years of growth and decay form a collision upon
fragmented space. between the earth and the body there is call to
stand immersed in its confines, counting the pedals and blades. as
you consider your position in this open pasture, counting the eroded
dams and gums, the direct presence of wind enters the lungs. the
absence of houses across these acres is essential to the landscape
as the vast and seemingly endless expanses of light call to you.
an ancient text written along the veins of the paddock presents a
scripture you learn to understand. the empty fence lines section
divisions in the farms you walk on. the sky is a growing peripheral
vision. day folds into day as rain signals the land's collapse in the
drive of another season, the paddocks face withers pulled along the
disposed fences frayed on the oval surfaces. when evening comes,
you trace the edges of the furthest paddock, circling the border in
a rigid line. hundreds of acres, where farmers have come before.
greyhound tracks like paths thread through the centre, crudely drawn
along the grasses. you come to a point where the periphery divides
into a road and gravel forks in a winding white line. no industry on
the side you stand on, footsteps framed as foreseen memory. men
come to die on the properties they grew up on, an eternal country,
drawn to depressions on the surface and the savagery of engrained
openness. from each side of the paddock the land enters you. the
flesh begins to understand what the mind cannot. you watch the
paddocks decay beneath the weight of houses. the construction of
time seeded in the dust remains, the earth opens and becomes the
fabric of the world.

The Uncertain Season

Wind breaks against the dam's edge,
a shadow falling slowly over the property.
night persists into the landscape, the thick branches of gums
obscuring the unveiling twilight.
smoke rises from a space in the grasses growing around the water
all distance sitting down inside the body.
I am alone.

the cold wind pierces the skin of my face
the language of the farmland driving the mind into a deeper silence
even when thinking of nothing at all.
thought alone can take you nowhere;

I sit here every night after school dreaming of
what lies beyond these paddocks,
tossing handfuls of dirt and rocks
into the shallow dam as crickets hum
in the reeds below the water.

I look out into the dark for hours.

Autumn Proverb

Walking the paddocks I saw a dog attack a bird,
take its fragile body in its jaws and shake it.
it lay motionless on the earth, the shrill cry that shattered the grasses
    fleeting.
I wondered what it must have thought of when its throat was torn,
who must now wait for its return, the coming of only a longer silence –

death, as absence, has a permanence the skin cannot repair,
captured in any moment that passes beneath a perfumed rain,
I recalled your ghost, transparent in the open paddock,
a thin veil of fog beginning to leak from the frame.

Passover

Any pasture welcomes decay,
skin worn in exposure
the horizon goes unseen at the crimson dawn.

body unrecognisable in the cold air
feeling of crossing the morning too quickly
and returning to the house.

you are not a part of this place.

Another Day at Home

Again it is dawn
the sound of water
against the dam's eroded basin.

at a careful distance from the deepest point
I press my hands into the tepid pool at its mouth,
the absence of heat pulsing faintly beneath my skin.

I cannot remember the rain or when it last fell

against the grasses.
I stare at the bone-coloured sky
surrounding the radiating sun
the paddock burning further into itself.

Shock Lessons, a Paddock Scripture

Exploring the farm as a child I would part the tall grasses,
moving through the dirt beneath the thick rushes.
consisting mainly of overgrown clover and clusters of foliage,
I'd map the distance that made up our property. it seemed endless,
that innocent drive to run further beneath the ceiling of leaves,
expanses of earth shifting beneath a child's slight weight.
I would imagine how far the landscape stretched.

one afternoon when my parents were at the races
I followed the pasture floor to the fence line at the back of the property.
wanting to go further, I hovered a blade of grass over the ticking wire
as I had watched Dad do so many times, to test if it was safe to cross.
feeling nothing, I wrapped my hands around one of the copper threads –
struck by that first surge through the body, electricity
running like a vein of blood beneath the skin
as though a voice screamed through a haze, blinding my eyes
and rattling my mind with panic.

no longer wishing to know more, to understand,
I stood startled at the trapped earth and wires
that had run a painful electric current through my body.
it would have been foolish to even attempt climbing
over into the neighbouring paddock.
all I could do then was give up.

Lines in Reflection

for my mother and father

The ways we have altered
as if time were shaping us
into a fully formed image of a family
indelible smoke emptying

from the weatherboard house
released into the clean air
I have used this image to rake
rocks from the driveway

to release the heavy breath
from the paddocks
below the urgency of it all
I have wished to remove all of it

to refashion your eyes
empty your bodies of the knots
building towards a fall
crossing the dams in hope of alterations

I can attempt to heal
beyond scars in the skin,
a depth without physical form
acres through Woodstock drying out

a calling up of memory
of your fathers, one five years dead
and one dying
shimmering and burning out

the lights from the house
became an endless blackness
even when calling to home
a sense of loss imagined

at the border of the property
the ancient gums cut the sky
clouds broken beneath the drive of wind
when death created inevitability

I followed your fear into it and did not return
the concrete rooftops called me to an edge
and stared down the years
then terror that allowed me to survive the height

veiled in secrecy, a slow drive
where reality was a confrontation unplanned
lit by the rooflights of the police car to a ward
with further assessments bearing my guilt

I was out of hospital
before you knew I had tempted an end
announced later after resurfacing
as I drew tears from your skin

you hated all the stages of waiting
as knowledge was a fear
I wondered how you saw weakness
and hated the very notion of suicide

the misunderstandings thinly built
by wind against the yellowing grasses
when I walked the paddocks
night after night in endless searching

a missing son love could not repair
and my apologies now
letting go of the embedded pain
accepting your arms, climbing further into you

towards a safety denied for years
that became too difficult to deem reality
regret escapes my wounds, divides amongst us
into a rebirth sounding from our property

I can now wake without withdrawing
into a state of anaemia
without freeing veins of blood from the body
handed to me from your mouths of optimism

all blood and flesh coupled, scarring
to present the skin in a new light
towards the body's flawing
as we love in unconditional manners
we must learn to take everything unscathed,
at whatever distance.

Farm Study

Nothing much ever happens.
a muteness that lies down in darkness
cleanly parted before the drive of rain
settling behind the mountains
the sculpted gums have long been fixed to the grasses.
before the breath can transcend the body
the shape of the sun multiplying behind the clouds
what does happen carves into memory
with unparalleled significance.

a horse attempting to break free of its paddock,
and flailing its head madly upon becoming tangled,
skin taut across the wire.

A Version of Hell

I often find I am walking further from myself, deeper into the property,
fingers pressed against the throat's basin to trigger an action,
the surface of my skin irreversible, my flesh starved of paradise –
I have shaped myself in ways I wish to bury beneath the present,

though unmistakably hell exists within the body –
it is written that dwelling within the inferno is the journey to become
    nearer
to faith, as I have not yet done
and I fear coming to a clearing centring the track
where nothing shines beyond

the compressed stomach of my life, like all perception, is broken
like waking amongst the grasses beneath the wires of dark rain,
all longing, all desire becoming a practice
where the self is only one version of hell –

always, I have things to look forward to
and pain to look back towards.

Bringing in the Greyhounds

Walking out to the runs

the dogs have been waiting for you

they bark at you and hope you pick them first.

For My Father, At Last

The paddocks couple with the sunlit clouds
and make you a landscape. transfusions of orange
setting behind the mountains
you walk the circled track
dogs of sand run beside you, the turf beneath a pale
mist expanded with grating weeds

down by the fence line the greyhounds start to climb
your arms, as much a part of you as I should be. the things
that alter on the property slip into memory
you foot the inconsistent slabs of sand as
the night comes past the cracked banks of the dams
eroded beside reeds floating in the water

always the revolving wind gathers all over the surface
of your face, your cold skin
worn away by years of work. it could be this side of dawn
that sees us meet in the track's centre. I weaken
as the grasses settle and turn into sleep
back at the house.

you stay out all night watching the sky
wishing it was already morning.

A Waking Farm

We will never know what they are barking at.
piercing the air at dawn
steadily they continue against the wind,
the persistent thread of breath
through wire.

To a Dead Poet

Charles Buckmaster, 1951–1972

A variation of waiting nothing coming

and the day
it is darker now

Woodstock. Gruyere. (Willochra)
abolished bastards of the trap a presence appears like a snare
apparitions are hallucinogenic pulses

ABSTRACTIONS RISE

the seed of god planted in the earth
but a disturbance...

the true nature of this fear?
brooding in its decayed
momentary time:
an isolation (not limited to poets).

of the WOMB destructive births
have entered.

WHITE WHALE COMING

great voiceless creature
we fled the city, belly
of the white whale filled
crushed grasses, grey buildings

state-wide MELBOURNE –
I visited your house
the school in Lilydale

couldn't find the broken poet
his aging disciple had stopped writing
died alone –

it is through leaving that our lives
begin to take form and enter full flight

writing poems across our skulls we
drink death, a kind of sweet wine.

The Colt's Grave

I stand at the paddock's edge
the colt's grave still visible
where dad has heaped wet dirt.

the ill and lanky body had fallen
several paddocks away, clean wind across the property
drying blood caked to his flanks.

a heartbeat ticking
through the electric fence
that formed a barricade around his small corpse

my father looking on
beyond my interminable confusion
inside my body, something changing

some future trying to enter the landscape.
I walk across the dilapidated horse track
waiting for the rain again.

from the weatherboard house
my breath is carried,
the unmistakable sound of crying.

Parkinson's

i.m. Jack Coburn

Terrifying
these empty days in fixation
not on your death but the way you died
the slow progression of rapture in the body
fracturing images
where the definition of muscle has diminished

in illness experience means little
cannot dictate composure
crossing from your eyes of war
long after the deaths of men you knew in youth and have forgotten
the faithless pulse of scars along the earth
where then your voice reduced to minimal protests for sleep

would rather you had left quickly
the ash palled on the paddocks' edge
from each direction light cast long
so that each blade was clear to you
from your unmoving shell

into seeing a culmination of flesh
the mechanical drag of skin as it tears
the way it must pull the taut face into stillness
and the long-drawn severity

still a strangeness in hoping to find you, before grief
where loss ignited your flight from pain
your eminent resign asked for
the scrawl of your hand distant in mine

all breath pitted against the skull
the separation of body, unresponsive years all
I have left of your name

the surge of blood
trailed off becomes a lull in consciousness
on your farm where I so often walk

grasses that flow gently
when all breath expires.

Reading the Paddock Scripture

Leaves fracture like glass
beneath your feet
the wind's pulse
driving through the open paddock.

somewhere
against the air's ceiling
you begin to draw a line
through the entries of your life.

an intercession thrown
against the landscape
in the hostile removal of the body

you live away now.
you do not see the trees.

nor the paddocks edge
drawing nearer
towards the depleting fields.

and you know, even at such distance, the body
will always be empty. you are waiting

as if the dirt could speak in reply.

How I Feel About Living Here

Back at the farm after days away
my father is in the shed mixing feeds
tearing open crude bags of mince.
the breath of dogs swoop through wire
and gather the scent at the forefront of bars,
bodies unfurl in kennels. the warm pressure

of dusk descends over the paddocks
the wind cutting through the tin
creating a breeze inside. his hands skirt easily
across the surface of the table.

this image – of dad opening the freezer
over and over sprinkling the kibble
into the mixed bowls then into the kennels
is one I know well. why am I still?
his body turning backwards
at my presence and walking straight up to me,
blood still dripping from his fingers –
I love all the things I hate about being here.

The Savagery of Thought

A man who wants to mutilate himself
is certainly damned, isn't he?
Arthur Rimbaud

The Nurse

I often ask for the ending.
blood-soaked white sheets you wake to each night
beneath their betrayed minds abandoned to your care.
I am sorry the body does not decide when.
and that you see me in the hollowed faces and knife-dreams.
not in your duty, all empathy soon becoming misery –
late one night you called through our silence,
a strange voice that spoke as if crying.
your mother was in another town asleep,
your father away at war, further from you than hours could say.
all distance finds loneliness in time.
I often ask for the ending.
no way to reassemble this.
no handbook or tested process written into your tongue.
only this strange voice I still hear
the night shift dragging to dawn
the mercy you breathe.

Night Turbulence

Writing beneath breath's turmoil, shadowed
leaves scrape against the window –

the disturbed light darkening the silent room.

The Savagery of Thought

The mirror is foreign
learning this language of the body, the ways it alters
in the throes of a deliberate brutality,

the savagery of thought, its driving influence over action,
harsh impressions left on the skin
as ash corrugates on the surface,
I climb into discolouration revelling in
the trance of pain, constructing a regressive agony,

standing before a transcendent reflection,
this language spoken in glass;
the physical dialect of my targeted body in the soft hum of blood –

harm is the cruel eye of the needle that the body threads through,
to ache is to witness being.

Convalescence

Because breath is only childhood
cowering in
      the belly of the hospital

the sound of his footsteps on the gravel
outside my bedroom window
      approaching the cages

and the endless thirst in me, seizing
my body and rupturing the bones.
      I blindly swallowed the days

the way a dog will run until it is lost
and I was never here

the medication, closer to nothingness
than ever being well.

myself, a stranger offering a space
      before the open window

my shadow contorting into
      the shape of my father.

Dementia

Before long nobody knows who you are;
body a stillborn, a bandaged voice
surrounded by an unending whiteness
screaming at someone coming after you.

somewhere dark a timeline appears
waiting to extinguish itself.
your dream to return to the demolished house
frightened by the sound of gunfire trying to wake you.

your narrowing eyes above the shadow
thrown from your mouth.
your hands did not move.
we waited for days in the reality of your waking,
the silence heavy as thought
caving against your skull.

Anorexia

The skin can be controlled
as any landscape can be altered.
greed swarming the belly.
wake. needlessly hungry. fat swelling around the jaw
and expanding the navel. the continuous growth of the mind –
the process of thought that breathes and contorts.
the other side of morning
entrenched in a stark vision of discipline.
the weight of meals is essential to measure.
the flesh sustained
without unnecessary interference.
the dream of starving. of disappearing
responding to each movement
overridden by
the drive of ambition.
you stand
lifeless
shrinking in the abandoned daylight.

Summertime

Pinned into my stomach, the wound
slowly heals, sadly
here in the summertime,
a rusted nail creaks beneath my flesh
scratched along the unnerved skin
this cycle bores me
heat batters the windows
still tired, serene daylight bent
against the encroaching frost
even when it is bright a charcoal
cloud grows and rains falls from
somewhere within
sweating against the inferno of sun
can't wear shirts anymore.

Letter

Distances have built this.
touching morning, briefly throwing
light across silences
numerous as hours.
impossible to believe
this was made by love
and this, too
is what trails the eyeless day
grieving and solitary,
clinging to something
unreachable.

The Face of My Arms

But the past forms so naturally.
an overrun of trees, thick spirals of branches
assembled in the centre of the paddock

the silence disappears
or like a periphery of abstractions
a mind walks across the body in the farmland's clearing

sits down, the body a landscape torn open
widening into distance

feels dark out here alone
already so full of hysteria
start with my arms
protruding veins of crumbled tissue
deadening the nerve ends

searching up and down
not for an image but an emptiness

the perpetual change stuns
risking yourself
in transfusions of a feeble red line

the point of beginning.

Skin

A surge of breath falls back into the wind, your hands poised and
    preparing dawn,
you release light into the day, the aerial smoke dissolves all around
    the body.
the still flow of grasses below the sky's ceiling follows a greying mist
    on charcoal paddocks.
through it no images enter my eyes but your figure readied in the pull
    of morning.

when I first met you, my flesh marred by decay and the turmoil you
    loved,
the strength of your gaze, innocent in its confusion and chaotic law
drove me forward, no emptiness allowing abandonment in a future
    we felt preparing.
I continued to return to you, finding your hesitation and mine in the
    danger
of a consuming desire, the panicking wind breaking against your face
    as memory,
and a lull in a truth we felt tracing our breath.

these ambitious tides submerging in the basin of the dams, your voice
softly rolling along the earth. void of exterior forces, still present in
your wild body, standing in defiance of death;
the unspeakable ache we share, hands we both wished to fend off in
    our innocence,
fanning the dark night from memory and resting in the finality of
    your gaze.

the drive of dark rain spirals onto the veranda at this distance,
regret at lacerations marked into my skin.
the pain fleeing from my flesh fractures beneath your action and
     because of you.
I am still drawn to the glowing landscape of your dream-life, your
     chaos
vanquishing mine and freeing us both, at last staring across the air
and seeing a future protruding through memory.

we sleep together here, my love of you despite myself, rebirth
as your beauty eases across a scarred mind.
the sudden flight of breath, my devotion prolonged in its urgency,
a collapse of light pours from your eyes, and I want to live.

Fervour

There are words that are never said.
we have no use of them.

the arrow lodged at the centre of time,
finding nothing

will not stop spinning.
direction does not concern

this brief use of breath. as at dusk

you never see light
fallen beneath the base of a tree.

Missing

Dawn comes   not unlike
the sleeplessness preceding it,
unalterable and dragging through your breath.

then there's the acute aloneness you have felt engraining anyway.

you walk on and pass through
an inexplicable view you search for
and watch fade perfectly from the periphery

your tongue fallen into deeper silence with each considered motion

thought itself is inconceivable

but you know at some point the grasses reach an end
and the pale tree-faces turn away.

the wind will start to dissolve skin.

look.

you are invisible as air.

She is Starving

Her body shrinks itself before morning.
the driving thoughts of bones disintegrating, burning
a hole into my mind. she wakes against her charred face

pulverised like her figure after the relapse.
does she hear the other side speaking to her
in the whispered tick of the scale building a bridge
to dawn. the house is still carpeted by her bones
even after sweeping and burning, blood marred
to slate, the voice has crushed her body against the walls.
after she collapsed
where was the ugly figure in the mirror then?
it did not reach out for her or grow. I ran my fingers over her wrists,
veins that could support a blade before food.
when her mother found her unconscious, she lived again
in a hospital in the city, I didn't know where to find it
or why she could not hear me calling.

face hollowed, balanced on weak pipe-cleaner limbs,
her skeleton breaks then aims to crumble
inside the dark's window. the floorboards snap her shrunken legs.
I carry the decaying white bones breathing in the unfurling
winds to the tomb her lifeless hands managed to prepare as
she starved, suiciding for years.

sleep now inside your skin of ghosts.
your voice will still trace my throat.
your absence will starve me
like a famine of memory.

Book Burning for Beginners

Each act of forgetting
sudden

from the striking of a match
to the flame's journey
across the pyres.

where heat can pierce skin –
all erasure a longing
conceived in fire.

The Invisible Sister

We have no hope and yet
we live in longing.
Dante Alighieri

1. The Doubled Question

The night sky is a blank, unbrushed canvas, early,
but slowly, the stars unfurl, collectives
scattered around the obscured half moon pushed
through the cloudy hue.
it does not revolve, stitched into the gold-flecked sky,
revealing circled edges every hour or so.
the dimly lit screen shows land beyond the window.
an open door is swung into place by the filtering winds,
the air is cooling outside and the trees sway with throes
of sleep. laying here awake, life is unchanged
yet in the vast air out there this same question we ask:
where are you?

2. Sororem

I woke from months of searching
at a distance that is unimportant.
my still dreaming mind walked a flat
and uninhabited stretch of road
past the hollowed gum trees lining her
property. the strobed lights were
like welcoming voices. her own children
asleep inside the house. a pulse bursting
inside me some night when the urgent
moon eclipsed the stars. I reached her
at the bay window in the front room
and stared from a distance that
distorted the aging features.

3. The Invisible Sister

I never met your mother
we swept light from eyes
each year blurred faces
bridges lengthened water shallow
we grow aware of each other
your name is all I have of your
mother and father together
the revolving game called searching
she hates him more than you could
sister still pray to meet today
I love blood from such distance.

Anorexia in Autumn

Image of autumn breaking against the trees
the vast expanses of light forming on the land's surface
fragments of this, and still, no substantial change.
a vision of physicality placed on the grasses.
     no reason for this starving feeling but control.

you are young.   your body withstands deprivation.

sectioning off the skin, the carrion-lined flesh that hungers
moving towards an ideal disappearance, even out here.

I like to touch your bones.
I like to watch you shrinking.
your figure is perfect

     when you lie back in the dark and no longer
belong anywhere.

Night Walk

I am not thinking, or walking for any reason

though I calculate these steps.
the madness in me
is breathing

in the silent hours
I see the air
does not belong to anyone, lost
against the freezing skin
I am still not tired enough
to sleep

and if my blood runs
it is not accidental

from where I am standing
the damaging is immeasurable

no one on the road at 4 am
listening
to the cars approaching.

Still Life with Suicidal Dream

It is daybreak
the faceless sun ignores sky
houses are empty
I drive down Whittlesea roads
never change people cloned

rivets down my arms
no pain anymore mark of pain
I used to feel

my mouth
always sounding in tremors
in response to eyes

road signs tell me what to do
where to go endless nowhere
continuing on through streets
boring never change

I dream of getting out
sleeping waking far from boring life

my forlorn head crushed
beneath the front tire who will drive over me
no one is aging people are foreign

this town an emptiness beyond words.

Pulse

Nothing here nothing changed
in the familiar columns of
houses

no shadow approaching in the
morning light
not you or anyone else.

not the greyed street corridors
the pulse of breath cowering
on the footpath and moving

across the whitening sky.
you could be anyone

no body or tongue caught
on a final word.

Lines to Myself

I wish you could see the rain for what it is;
not as a tense progression in mood or a reason
to feel something.
the ache pressing against your temples has no
connection to this atmosphere.

the cold wires striking the roof of the car
above your head muffle the sound of traffic
progressing down the roads in the distance.

and you are sitting here alone again, imagining
how long the hours will take to slip past you
until you can drive home and
wait for tomorrow.

you must understand your mind is not your own.
the emergence of fear settling into your breath
is not a fault of character, not weakness.
and this imbalance is beyond your control.

it can't always be this way,
packing your books and driving north
avoiding the ones who love you,
seeking distance from your thoughts
inside this dark shell.

I can promise you something.

one day, as if the instant between
catastrophe and rebirth could vanish
you will recognise something new about
the image distorting in the wet glass.
I tell you, now,

you won't always be so unwell.

Before Dawn

Only this voice that thrusts you
into consciousness
nobody here in the silent house
but the past and your mother's eyes
filled with distance as a form of love.
the soft morning rain,
sole light from the lamp over the desk
and no words to set down
to rewrite your life into beauty.
this constant reopening of memory
of yourself five years ago
possessed by that blind drive to continue
walking along the rooftop
the distant concrete looming below
before the sectioned breath collapsed
and again led you to life.

Rebirth

I prepared my flesh for its new life yesterday
steadied the crudely fashioned handles and pulled
quickly.

the rip left sheets of scar tissue emptying
onto the carpet, a stain forming a puddle beneath
my naked white toes.

the torn opening widened into a hole where
my mouth had been, sprawled still across the
floor.

the scarred surface shed its habit and
abandoned its blemishes easily
falling through the circled and frayed furrows.

after the burning of dawn tanned the leathery
skin, the old body collapsed in a heap of bone
and sinew, each stage of decomposition
breathing through my sewn throat where breath
bled from my bare lungs.

in the building light I watched drawn wires
tangled across the line of pegs as I secured
the other flesh to dry out:
it fit better and wore itself in around
my glad eyes and abraded insides.

this was the beginning, the new became
normal before darkness could be heightened,
loosened into the clear shot of morning.

Starless Sky

A weathered skeleton
in windy fields of memory,
piercing like a knife
Matsuo Basho

Starless sky
the black cord
to the fuse box

The cooling dusk
a man boards the train
in the wrong direction

dusk entering the dog's eyes peer through the wire

again answering
the telephone to silence
Summer rain

Packing my life
into a cardboard box
persistent rain

Distant acres
the stale wind through
the gum tree's branches

What remains of my childhood
the dam eroded
at its deepest point

First day of Summer
the weatherboard house
without him

Swaying moth orchids...
the dead singer's voice
from the speakers

Night darkening —
the old tin silo
only a shadow

Autumn wind
the greyhound
outruns my father

Separation   in the barren paddock only the stars

Race day
the young greyhound
examines its paw

A break in the rain some of the grasses flattened

Dawn without rain
a phone call
from a stranger

First winter rain
running my hands
over his collar

First day of winter
on the veranda
a black dog wakes

Crimson sky
overgrown trees obscure
the path I search for

Hare

I will give you a new heart and put a new spirit in you;
I will remove from you your heart of stone
and give you a heart of flesh.
Ezekiel 36:26

Ceremonial / For Hare

In the earth itself there is no morning,
darkness without end, as if sleeping
no blank dawn, no promise
of deepening hunger
inside the innumerable frames
bound in directionless motion.
before absolute pain can rise
into seeing mercy in the slipstream
of distance –
someday, you will be here.

Calvary

So we are surrounded.
one day I hope you will see it.
it still feels like only yesterday I was with you
younger and slightly more afraid
waiting up all night in the blackened bedroom
turning away again and again
from the tortured icon
hanging on the wall
desperately trying
to trap you in my hands.

Hanged Rabbit / Torch Song

*

A dream, Hare, long ago,
           with all words that reveal I passed
through this world. in the dawn where
           the echoes begin. where they end.

*

           Distance felt like touching skin
celestial murmurs entered the day like thunder,
           all ardour vanishing into the deepening morning,
colours softened, monochromatic sky, eyes filmed over and passing
           as stark images of seraphim becoming stone.
behind my mind's torched recollection of footsteps from the street's
    edge
           behind you as you disappear into the gathering of people
               lining the city.
not that I could not have followed –
           disintegration and stillness. gesture of the granite path
leading to an unfamiliar division of Babylon,
           in an instant we could pass one another,
strangers.

*

I was sure I was wounded.
		no blame had set its place for you,
blackened sky across the grey city
		a struck match could not light –
I was certain blood was the flesh in its flight of longing, as Charles
	had written.
		dying was just the next poem I would write, Hare.
intermittently balanced between sleep and inebriation,
		prayer's silent answer. and nothingness. no longer revulsion.
the baited shadow of your featureless gaze
		the naked body becoming me
where intimacy burned and terminated into lifeless memory
		Hare, Hare, Hare, tell me now how a beginning is eventual
in each arrival when you have returned home, where the silence is
	unending
and it is dawn forever.
		a voice inside me murmured
not tonight
		but I continually felt the walls forcing my body
from the frame, ceaseless burning of our birth bound into this
	redemption
		I contemplated regret and the passage of forgiveness,
the stillness of language and insignificance of my own breath
		shallow upon my tongue.
to which extent anguish forsook me.
		not death, as you had also lived
days away now. towers of glass on the tables as all conversation
	collapsed

sex returned, the vast hunger unravelling and clawing the
       dry air
I came to you when you called each time.
       inaudible promise guiding aversion into an impulse
mouth of the train station swallowing me where I waited all night
       body beside me waking to a new darkness;
you sleeping alone or with another, it no longer mattered.

*

       Stillness, Hare. absolution unmoving and rapture eternal,
 in the carrying of the dead child that rests
       beneath His kingdom.
the bones beginning to speak inside me.
       to leave, to live, only
I could not move, not without your eyes becoming a pair of hands
       in the great quiet surrounding me. no.
blindness and the father's betrayal come.
       I am lost, Hare. your voice clawing into the silent
and unwinding night and rooting in the undergrowth.
       your body resting there and venturing nowhere.
tell me, Hare, that purposeless desire leading to an abysmal depth is
   abject.
       book, spoken of in your tongue only abasing me, unreservedly.
He will come, imminent judgement and love indistinguishable.
       there is a vengeance in you, I see it.

night of flesh palled without consequence.
      the tasteless dark, death and His glory.

*

returning, we made love.
      harsh light and my head of ethanol
in poverty's unendurable grasp, our hell shifting.
      your body sprawled across the bed afterwards, as you slept
invoked the ghost of the rabbits my grandfather had hung across the wire
      at the front of our property when I was a child.
bleeding out, tawdry noose erected by our family Abel, the soul's
  unreachable divinity.
      He watched, I remember, Hare.
Lord, not here or anywhere. I wept openly, carving your doctrine
into childhood's clear flesh and understood
      how we each know our crucifixion
how He made violence from nothing.
      a pulse of blood rises in your chest and will not stop sounding
      around me
your still figure against the linen and haired rabbit-shadow
      across the ashen walls.
Hare, I love you so honestly I am fearful,
      His child cowering beneath the frail birch trees,
the flame, loveless room of reconciliation, the word.

*

the gate cannot open nor is death the key.
      I am telling you, Hare.
each hour hunted, the unending fire clinging to nothingness,
      blind Messenger and the impossible future
revealed in the sacrificial light, blanketed,
      you will remember, judgement.
Hare, hear me.
      meditation of vision, and genesis of love forgotten
we will be dust in unfurling winds, ether
      and this formless dawning, damnation,
driving black rain and sin, drowned words,
      our insurmountable life
and understanding your leaving, Hare; as it recurs in my mind,
      and is still yet to happen.

Eve

And being thankful to have lived -
a harsher exposure, unparalleled in the unmoving, clean air
night sky radiating beneath the world's
stained ceiling.
the familiar drive to leave
the crying child at the gate's mouth

watched the light receding from the blade's edge
and walked again from the garden
into the unknowable border of hope

wishing to no longer be afraid
this scarred earth I cannot see
but know entirely
days terminated here,
the empty room and arc
I can never board
moored between this world and the next

words without form, birth's cruelty
and your faceless voice reaching
into the nothingness that wakes in me
all longing stitched into skin, shifting and eaten away until

I again shield my eyes;
the incomprehensible weight of the sky
towards the body's unceasing prayer
to resign and be destroyed.

the collapsed childhood replaced
as the will to live
becomes its breath.

Summer's End

Then the acres themselves burning,
blades of yellowed grass
against stale air,
naked branches moving against the drying wind.
perhaps you do not remember.

can only imagine dying here
as if you were the only one waiting
all your life to know
where the body will rest.
your words like rain driving
through the farmland's clearing
when I was only five years old.

perhaps you do not remember.
your voice drawn back
from the paddock's edge
where I am no longer a child
no longer fear you;
remember, when I die

I will call your name
like it is blood in my mouth.

Testament

No moment of permanence, the rubble
        mounting. now the stars piercing the city's surface.
I know you, child of faceless terror.
        day's unceasing orbit, where the dead wait.
and words you murmured in the black hallways
        of our fragile movement.
my God, I can't bear the earth in its mirrored vulnerability.
        your familiar abandonment; the desire again
to draw blood from my body, to examine its machinery,
        how I may know the dead as you do
a hallowed dark thread into this unseemly consciousness
        I again choose. it is all baseless,
the will to harm and be forgiven these excavations
        and needless betrayals, the forceful closing
of the wound's mouth, not the wish for death itself, as you know it,
        only acceptance of Glory-made depressions
in the earth's skin. Again it is not you who sees the beauty of mercy
        when it is no longer there.

Woodstock Parable

The night will be mounted like a canvas
of beginning when you wake
vines like rosary coveting the sleeping farmhouse
as you fold your hands, shivering
in the winter morning
sightless, the cold wind from the earth
secured on its revolving axis
like herons circling the open paddocks, Hare.
unnamed, you will witness reckoned panic
in the arteries of the past unfurling,
mouthfuls of sunlight and the drive to not be ill.

Father of this unendurable forgiveness I know,
hear me.

Stigmata

To awaken is to accept being again regardless of circumstance, the hunted hours in the framework of the day perturbed as the memory of native birth; the slashed tongue of a lamb discolouring the water of its drinking sisters as it prolonged its flight back towards the earth, her urgent bleating itself seeming to pool in the stained tin basin. and for all this I am lost, Lord.

I am sorry for my cowardice and my hours terminated in the drained rivers of the city when I have known my health and chosen to dwell only in my fog. Insurmountable forgiveness, the sick child waking terrified in the morning air; and the stark image of weeping hands, of thorns, a nail driven into the dawn.

Baptism

And I still know nothing of you since your leaving. nothing, a hell of
my own invention glimpsed from the assuaged anguish of morning.
in the dawn arriving unaware of the night. a vacant sky heavy with
the loss of your unknowable language, all notions of desire empty.
I am incomprehensibly weak. my failure in loving your body alone
and knowing the broken flesh of others, asking for the murderer in
me who urgently waits. a closeness in my blood you offer to me as the
hunger comes to despairingly sacrifice my body. again I will pray to
be dust and you will let me be here.

Poem for an Orchid

The fragility of knowing one another
        is a furrow I make in your body, Hare.
my determined excarnation amidst
        our grassless summer, altering
in the barren paddock's mouth,
        counterbalanced between
your craning neck and the sky.
        there your ghost has been seeking
my open hands,
        this stark and concealed vulnerability
of all that lives in your viscera where I love you
        as I have loved all I cannot touch and pray for.
I long one day to walk your broken earth, Hare,
        to not apologise for being here.

Acknowledgements

Grateful acknowledgement is made to the editors of the following
publications in which most of these poems first appeared, sometimes
in slightly different forms: *5 Poems* (Donnithorne Street Press, 2015),
Bareknuckle Poet, Before Bone and Viscera (Rochford Street Press, 2014),
*Blithe Spirit, Bluepepper, The Canberra Times, Cordite, Creatrix, Echidna
Tracks, ETZ, foam:e, Four Hundred and Two Snails* (Haiku Society of
America, 2018), *Frogpond, Hedgerow, Island, Mad Songs* (Blank Rune Press,
2015), *Mascara Literary Review, Meanjin, Modern Haiku, Otoliths, Overland,
Poetry, Presence, The Silences* (Eaglemont Press, 2016), *StylusLit, To End All
Wars* (Puncher & Wattman, 2018), *Verity La, Wales Haiku Review, Westerly,
Windfall, The Wonder Book of Poetry, Writ Poetry Review, Writing to the Wire*
(UWA Publishing, 2016).

My sincere gratitude also to Robert Adamson, Michele Seminara,
Anthony Lawrence, Ivy Alvarez, Elizabeth Campbell, Amanda Joy,
Peter Minter, Ian McBryde, Carmen Main, Joel Deane, Amanda Anastasi,
Anthony O'Sullivan, Luke Best, Melinda Smith, Peter Jeffrey, Ron Moss,
π. O., Sandy Caldow, Harriet Jarrett and Lou Verga for their advice,
encouragement and support. Thank you also to my family and friends.